POPE J

THE GOOD POPE

About Wyatt North Publishing

Starting out with just one writer, Wyatt North Publishing has expanded to include writers from across the country. Our writers include college professors, religious theologians, and historians.

Wyatt North Publishing provides high quality, perfectly formatted, original books.

Send us an email and we will personally respond within 24 hours! As a boutique publishing company we put our readers first and never respond with canned or automated emails. Send us an email at hello@WyattNorth.com, and you can visit us at www.WyattNorth.com.

Foreword

John XXIII was nicknamed "The Good Pope" because of his humble, loving, and open character and his gracious sense of humor. In possessing those attributes, he is viewed by many to be similar to Pope Francis today.

Like Pope Francis, Pope John was wont to stroll about Rome by night and make pastoral visits to sick children and prison inmates. John's secretary, the Italian prelate Loris Capovilla, heard the news from Pope Francis himself and remarked how appropriate it was for the step to be taken by "the successor most similar" to John.

Shortly before Pope John's death, the International Balzan Foundation, which is headquartered in Milan and Zurich, awarded Pope John its Peace Prize. Then, in December 1963, President Lyndon Johnson posthumously awarded him the United States' Presidential Medal of Freedom, the nation's highest civilian award.

The canonization of Pope John XXIII was announced by Pope Francis shortly after the fiftieth anniversary of John's death. The date for canonization has been set for April 27, 2014, Divine Mercy Sunday, the first Sunday after Easter.

Table of Contents

"I have looked into your eyes with my eyes. I have put my heart near your heart."

An Introduction

The year was 1958. Pope Pius XII, who had ascended the papal throne on the eve of WWII and had continued to lead the Church through the beginnings of the Cold War, was dead. As though unsure of which direction to take in an uncertain world, the College of Cardinals opted for an interim pope. Nearly 77 years old, Cardinal Roncalli was aged even by papal standards.

In some ways, the recently deceased pope and the newly announced one could not have been more different. Whereas Pope Pius had come from an aristocratic lineage long tied to the papacy, Roncalli was of undistinguished peasant stock. Nevertheless, Roncalli had acquitted himself admirably in difficult positions of responsibility and would make an acceptable caretaker pope, one who could be counted on for a quietist attitude of maintaining the status quo. That was not what happened.

The papacy of Pope John XXIII lasted a brief four years and seven months, yet in that time, Pope John succeeded in bringing about a sea change in how the Church interacted with the modern world and its inhabitants. A great-hearted man of profound compassion, Pope John wanted the Church to meet the changing needs of the people that comprised his global flock and, perhaps even more importantly, to act with higher regard for those that were not a part of his Church. The most remarkable thing about

Angelo Roncalli was how open his heart was to all people. This was no affectation; he genuinely liked people, and they, in turn, would find that they loved him.

Background

Angelo Giuseppe Roncalli was born on November 25, 1881, the fourth of fourteen children, several of whom died in childhood. He was the eldest son of Giovanni Battista Roncalli and Marianna Mazzola Roncalli, who were poor tenant farmers. The family resided, as it had for hundreds of years, in the tiny farming village of Sotto il Monte ("Under the Mountain"), seven miles from the city of Bergamo in the Italian Alps. As Angelo would later put it, the family was poor in material goods but rich in faith.

They lived meagerly in an extended-family household that included a large host of cousins—twenty-eight people altogether at the time Angelo was born. The bachelor great-uncle Zavario Roncalli presided as patriarch over the family, conducting nightly rosary and pious readings. The family was too poor for meat or bread and so usually subsisted on polenta. The two-story, 300-year-old farmhouse where they all lived had no running water or fireplaces. In winter, the farm animals were kept on the first floor, making their rising body warmth available to the people living in the upper story as had been done throughout the Mediterranean regions since biblical times.

When Angelo was nine, they moved to a much larger, better farmhouse with eighteen rooms. Eventually, after many years, the family would rise from abject poverty to purchase that house and the small bit of land they farmed.

Young Angelo, known at that age as Angelino, began his education at a one-room village schoolhouse with three benches, one for each grade. School was taught by the parish priest, Don (Father) Francesco Rebuzzini. One of the younger Roncalli brothers would later marvel in recollection that Angelo actually wanted to go to school. That difference between them, the brother surmised, was why he himself remained illiterate, while his brother had gone on to become pope.

In this first stage of his education, Angelo so sufficiently distinguished himself that it cost him a beating. On one occasion, a visiting district supervisor of schools posed a trick question to the children: Which weighed more—a measure of iron or a measure of straw? Angelo was the only child to realize that there was no difference in the measurement, so "we beat him up," recalled his childhood classmate. It was an environment in which excellence was viewed with suspicion and standing out provoked petty jealousies.

When Angelo had gone as far as he could in the local school, Don Francesco convinced Giovanni to send his son to a nearby parish for Latin training from the priest there. The boy was taught Latin using Caesar's *Gallic Wars*. He later jokingly estimated that for each page he learned, he earned one clout from the priest. Angelo was nearly ten when Don Francesco coaxed Giovanni into allowing his son to progress to a secondary school about five miles distant.

Times were changing, the priest told the father; a boy with ability needed an education. At first, Angelo stayed near the school with other relatives, but his mother soon fetched him away from that squabbling environment, and he then had to walk the five miles over a mountain to school each day. He was so exhausted from the long walk each way that he was not able to learn well. In addition, the other students made fun of the country boy with his poor clothes and funny speech.

Despite the boy's poor performance at the secondary school, Don Francesco continued to champion him and won Angelo admission to the junior seminary in Bergamo, which had been founded by Saint Charles Borromeo. The year was 1892, and Angelo was not yet eleven years old. He struggled with math and some other subjects in Bergamo, but over time, he began to excel in his studies, particularly showing a predilection for history and theology.

He was barely fourteen in 1895, when, probably at the behest of his teachers, he began to keep a spiritual journal, which he would continue throughout his lifetime. In it he chronicled his inward struggle for sanctity, and in reading his journals, one can discern his intellectual, spiritual, and emotional development over time. The first entry was piously entitled, "Rules of life to be observed by young men who wish to make progress in the life of piety and study." It was followed by such categories as resolutions, spiritual notes, maxims, and reflections. The lifetime collection was later published as *Journal of a Soul,* and it affords us a unique chronicle of the spiritual journey of a young seminarian up through his priesthood and on to the papacy.

Although he loved his family and remained quite close with them throughout his life, young Angelo would feel less at home in Sotto il Monte as time passed. His education at the seminary in Bergamo was gradually setting him apart. At the age of fourteen, he received the tonsure, creating a further distinction from those around him. Villagers treated the youth with increased respect and distance. And then, with so many people living together at home, it was only natural that quarrels would emerge. Angelo found the petty bickering to be a trial, particularly as he was working to elevate his own soul. As a result, his cousins felt he put on airs, and some found him arrogant.

When Angelo became aware of their hostile sentiments, he began a spiritual battle to suppress these traits. Nevertheless, at this point in his life, visits home were challenging for him. It was difficult both for the boy and the family to balance his youth with his ascending status.

The Young Priest

In 1901 Angelo and two other promising young men from the Bergamo seminary received scholarships for further study at the Pontifical Seminary, known as the Apollinaire, in Rome. Because of his youth, he was required to begin his study of theology again from the beginning. Angelo was in his element surrounded by history and the pilgrimage sites of his faith. He immersed himself in his studies and the rarified atmosphere of Rome. Clergy, however, were not exempt from the Italian military at that time, and after only one year of study in Rome, he was drafted and had to return to Bergamo to serve in the infantry. For a year he exchanged his cassock for a different type of uniform.

Life in the barracks was jarring after his insular life in the seminary, but the earthy and sometimes vulgar interests of his military companions broadened his life experience. His outgoing nature won him many friends, and he found that most of the men he encountered respected his clerical status. (He would later be recalled to active duty, and in that second military experience, he had to cope with more disapproving officers.) He was promoted to the rank of corporal and became a sergeant shortly before his discharge.

Having completed his military service in November 1902, Angelo returned to his studies and achieved a doctorate in sacred theology. In August 1904, when he was not quite the required age of twenty-three, Angelo Roncalli was ordained in Rome. He said his first Mass the following day in St. Peter's Basilica and was later presented in audience to Pope Pius X, who blessed his good intentions. He then returned home to Sotto il Monte so that he could say Mass in the presence of his proud family. Following theses joyful events, he resumed his studies at the Seminario Romano, working towards an additional doctorate in canon law.

In January 1905 Pope Pius X asked the young priest from Bergamo to assist in the consecration ceremony for Bishop Giacomo Radini-Tedeschi, who was about to assume leadership of the Bergamo diocese. The new bishop was impressed with Father Angelo and appointed him to be his secretary. Father Angelo served as the bishop's secretary for nearly ten years until the vigorous bishop's premature death at the age of fifty-seven. During that time, at the bishop's suggestion, he also assumed a post in the Bergamo seminary as a theology professor. He taught classes in patrology, apologetics, and Church history, and he was a popular teacher. In addition, he began research on an ambitious multi-volume work on Saint Charles Borromeo, the last volume of which was not published until after he became pope. With this multitude of roles, Father Angelo began to flex his pastoral muscles, and he did so under the socially progressive tutelage of Monsignor Radini-Tedeschi.

Father Angelo was utterly devoted to his bishop, later calling him his "polar star." Monsignor Radini was from an aristocratic family and had served as a Vatican diplomat. He moved comfortably among the higher echelons of the Church, and wherever he went, he was accompanied by his young shadow. With Monsignor Radini, Father Angelo traveled for the first time outside of Italy: to pilgrimage sites in France and then to countries throughout Europe and, in 1906, to the Holy Land. He also visited every parish in the diocese of Bergamo because Monsignor Radini was not one to sit idly—he was a leader of the Catholic Action movement in Italy and was especially concerned about the rights of workers, which had been recently articulated in Pope Leo XIII's 1891 *Rerum Novarum* (*On Capital and Labor*). Monsignor Radini believed in an activist Church that pursued the earthly fight for social justice, and he regularly met with like-minded people.

Father Angelo had earlier been attracted to such ideas, but now he was exposed to the foremost activist thinkers of the Church, and he had the opportunity to witness how their ideas could be practically applied. Among the other programs Monsignor Radini put in place was an office for assisting poor Italian émigrés seeking employment outside the country. During a contentious strike at the large iron foundry in Ranica, Monsignor Radini's involvement prompted complaints to the Vatican. He and Father

Angelo opened soup kitchens and provided money to the strikers' relief fund among their other support for the workers.

Following the bishop's untimely death from colon cancer in 1914, mere days after the death of Pope Pius X and only months after the outbreak of WWI, Father Angelo moved out of the bishop's palace. The loss of "my bishop" was extremely difficult for him. By now he had grown close with his family again and often sought consolation in visits with them. He continued to teach in the Bergamo seminary and to serve as a pastor.

This activity was interrupted when he was recalled to active military duty upon Italy's entry into WWI in 1915. He served first as a sergeant in the medical corps. Bergamo was a receiving station for the wounded coming from the front lines. As a medical orderly, Sergeant Roncalli saw a tremendous amount of human suffering. When he could no longer physically help a wounded soldier, he came to the soldier's aid as a priest, comforting and administering last rites. A year later priests in the Italian military were finally made chaplains, and he was promoted to the rank of lieutenant. Having trained at the side of Monsignor Radini, Lieutenant Roncalli energetically took spiritual charge of the diverse hospitals and schools that were housing the wounded. He established an association to aid the female relatives of deceased soldiers and a convalescent home for wounded soldiers.

The decision to enter the war was catastrophic for Italy. By war's end, some 600,000 Italians would be killed and nearly one million wounded. In the Roncalli family, Angelo's four brothers also served in the military, leaving the women and the aged males to farm the land. Angelo was naturally worried about his brothers at the front. In the rare moments when he was able to be alone, the wasteful destruction of life sometimes brought him to tears. A cousin on the Mazzola (maternal) side of the family died of wounds from an Austrian grenade. And following the disastrous battle at Caporetto—one of the worst defeats in all military history—Angelo's youngest brother, Giuseppe, was reported missing in action. His family feared the worst. Giuseppe would eventually reappear as a prisoner-of-war held by Austria and live to return home, but one of the daughters of the family, Enrica, died of cancer at the tragic age of twenty-five, only a few weeks before the end of the war.

When the war finally did end, Father Angelo opened a Student House at the behest of the now-bishop of Bergamo, Monsignor Marelli. It was intended to serve the spiritual needs of young people. Since the bishop was low on funds because of the war, Father Angelo used his own discharge pay and money borrowed from his father to set up the facility, which provided meals, housing, a quiet place for study, and a recreational area. He brought two of his sisters, Ancilla and Maria, to be housekeepers and help run the hostel. Father Angelo had become accustomed to helping his family in whatever ways he could, often using his meager salary to pay for doctors, food, and other necessities. In particular, he took responsibility for the upkeep of these two unmarried sisters.

In 1919 Father Angelo also became spiritual director of the Bergamo seminary, but he was not asked to teach, perhaps because of suspicions that he was too progressive. Father Angelo grew happy again. He was settling into a future working with young people when the Vatican stepped in.

Leaving Italy

At this point, the career path of Angelo Roncalli exemplifies how passing contacts can result in career advancement. After the death of Bishop Radini-Tedeschi, Father Angelo decided to compose a biography of his beloved mentor. He was somehow able to complete it during the war years and sent a copy to Pope Benedict XV, who had been a close friend of the bishop's. After the war, in 1920, Pope Benedict remembered Father Roncalli and removed the priest from Bergamo, appointing him a director of the organization for the support of foreign missions, the Society for the Propagation of the Faith (Propaganda Fide). Although it was a minor position, he met a number of important Church figures throughout Europe and began to be known to the hierarchy in Rome. Now, as a domestic prelate, he was able to add red piping to his garb, the significance of which puzzled his family, and was entitled to be called "monsignor."

In addition, because of his earlier association with Monsignor Radini, he had met a librarian in Milan, Monsignor Achille Ratti, who later became Pope Pius XI. The contact had led Father Roncalli to discover the material he would use for his biography of Saint Charles Borromeo, and the librarian gave his permission and advice about how to proceed. Later, as pope, Pius XI appointed Monsignor Roncalli to the Vatican diplomatic service. Roncalli was made an archbishop and named apostolic visitor to Bulgaria in March 1925.

In truth, the new archbishop was not happy with his assignment to Bulgaria. A Lombard to the bone, he did not wish to leave Italy, his native region of Lombardy, or his family. Since it would not be feasible to bring his two sisters along, he further had to ponder the difficult problem of their disposition while he was abroad for an indeterminate period. In the end, he rented part of a large house in Sotto il Monte for his sisters, and this became his summer home through all the years until he became pope.

Adding to Angelo's unhappiness at leaving Italy was the fact that he was genuinely frightened; he did not believe himself to be a capable enough person to assume this new status. He thought himself lazy and untalented, so he resolved to rely upon God for help. If it were God's desire that he become an archbishop and go to Bulgaria, surely God would make up for his shortcomings. He took as his episcopal slogan *Obedientia et Pax*, Obedience and Peace.

Monsignor Roncalli had not wanted or sought this type of advancement. What is more, there had been no papal representative in Bulgaria in 500 years. So why did it happen? Some have speculated that Pope Pius moved Angelo to Bulgaria in order to remove him from Italy. Pius XI was a disappointment to many in Italy because he failed to live up to progressive expectations and made a shocking alliance with Mussolini. Monsignor Roncalli was a known supporter of the Catholic Popular Party, which Pius suppressed in favor of the Italian fascists.

It is true that by appointing him to Bulgaria, Pope Pius effectively put the monsignor's suspect views on the shelf and segregated him, even while making him a titular archbishop. But just as the biblical Joseph was required to become a slave in Egypt for a time before rising to the lofty role God intended for him, God also had future plans for Angelo Roncalli. And as time passed and Mussolini's fist tightened around Italy, Archbishop Roncalli would come to view it as a blessing that he had been able to leave.

And so Archbishop Roncalli found himself aboard the Orient Express on his way to Sofia. Bulgaria was an obscure outpost for the Catholic Church. Archbishop Roncalli's job there was to protect the interests of the small Catholic community in the predominantly Eastern Orthodox country. Fortuitously, he was also able to provide broader assistance during two national tragedies, thereby attaining a great deal of good will from the Orthodox majority.

The first event occurred even before his arrival. Nine days before the new archbishop arrived in Bulgaria, an attempt was made to assassinate the king of Bulgaria, Boris III, by placing a bomb in the dome of Sofia's main Orthodox cathedral. The horrific explosion caused the dome to crash down upon the congregants, killing 150 people and injuring 300. Arriving in Bulgaria so soon after the terrible event, the new papal visitor visited the wounded in a Catholic hospital that provided free care in the aftermath of the calamity. Archbishop Roncalli's ecumenical kindness so favorably impressed King Boris that he received the archbishop only days later. This was an especially meaningful gesture on the part of the king because the papal visitor had no actual diplomatic standing in the country.

The second occasion was in 1928, when Bulgaria experienced a series of destructive earthquakes. Archbishop Roncalli directed food and blanket distribution in the decimated earthquake areas, and he even elected to sleep among the homeless in tents. In addition, he solicited funds for a soup kitchen that fed people for two months following the catastrophe.

Archbishop Roncalli also gained favor with the royal family by overlooking King Boris' somewhat duplicitous behavior in connection with the Catholic Church. In 1930 this king of Orthodox Bulgaria had married Giovanna, the Catholic daughter of King Victor Emmanuel III of Italy, in a Catholic ceremony in Assisi. Archbishop Roncalli was present for the occasion. The pope had granted the couple the customary dispensation when they both signed a promise that any issue from their marriage would be reared as Catholics. Nevertheless, upon their arrival in Bulgaria, the couple was remarried in a spectacular Orthodox ceremony, which the pope suffered as a slap in the face.

The children that followed were baptized Orthodox, further angering the pope. Archbishop Roncalli accepted Giovanna's word that she had no say in the matter, and he understood enough of realpolitik to recognize that Boris, too, had little choice in this regard: to keep the wavering support of the Orthodox Bulgarian populace, Boris could hardly show weakness in his Orthodoxy. As it was, he was the frequent target of assassination attempts in his simmering country, and he did eventually die in 1943 at the age of 49 under highly suspicious circumstances.

While Roncalli did favor reconciliation and reunification of the Catholic and Orthodox Churches, his mission in Bulgaria was not to be an emissary to the Orthodox but to assist the Catholics there. The majority of Catholics in Bulgaria were in fact already well served by two bishops. These were Catholics of the Latin rite, mostly foreigners living in the chief population centers of

Bulgaria. In addition, however, there were some 14,000 Uniates who followed Orthodox liturgy and customs but at the same time were in union with the Vatican. They were mostly poor and lived in rural regions without the benefit of hierarchical oversight.

Having trained under the tutelage of Bishop Radini-Tedeschi, Archbishop Roncalli followed the lead of his mentor and went out to seek his constituency. He travelled broadly throughout the countryside to wherever they could be found—by car, wagon, and mule. He was accompanied on his journeys by a young Uniate priest, Stefan Kurtev. The simple people the archbishop visited were often astonished to receive such a high-ranking visitor as the archbishop.

Having previously worked with Catholic missions, Roncalli was already sensitive to the question of Church-sponsored colonialism. Thus he felt it was important for the Uniates to have their own, indigenous leadership, and he recommended Father Kurtev be appointed a bishop. The Vatican would eventually allow this but only after considerable foot-dragging. Archbishop Roncalli also sought to create a Uniate seminary for the development of a local priesthood, but although he succeeded in purchasing the property for it, he was never allowed to commence building. The Vatican's failure to support his endeavors both puzzled and hurt him, and he continually struggled with a lack of clarity and direction for his mission in Bulgaria. There remained no clear message from Rome concerning what exactly it was he was supposed to accomplish. He longed to minister directly to the folk of the land, but there was no forum for him to do so.

In all, the ten years in Bulgaria (1925–1934) were often discouraging and lonely for an energetic and dedicated man in his prime, but Archbishop Roncalli endured them with fortitude and good humor. His next appointment was equally obscure: apostolic delegate to Greece and head of the Vatican diplomatic mission to Turkey. Since Greece, too, was predominantly Eastern Orthodox, while Turkey was Muslim or secular, he again presided over many small communities in somewhat hostile settings. Nevertheless, his naturally friendly personality and bountiful good sense won over many friends. Istanbul, where the archbishop resided, did have a large Catholic community so that the archbishop finally had his own cathedral and the opportunity to engage in the pastoral duties he had missed for so long. The communities he served were extremely diverse so that he had to negotiate among churches in communion with Rome but adhering to their own very different traditions.

The secular Turkish government of the time was ruthless in asserting its authority over any survivors of Islamic rule. As such, it also moved to suppress other religions. Clergy were not permitted to wear clerical garb, so the archbishop had to wear regular suits when out and about. Since the government also closed the diocesan newspaper, the archbishop's attempts to communicate with his audience were somewhat circumscribed. Undaunted, he reached out to the ecumenical patriarch of Orthodoxy even though healing relations was not then on the Vatican agenda. He also established friendly relations with any and all foreign diplomats present in Istanbul. In a foreshadowing of his future moves as pope, he introduced the use of Turkish for all parts of the liturgy that weren't mandatorily said in Latin. It became necessary for him to defend that practice when he was denounced to the Vatican because of it.

Meanwhile, the political crisis in Europe was escalating with growing rapidity. Pius XI, in failing health, finally grasped the full, horrible meaning of Nazism and in early 1937 issued an encyclical against it, *Mit Brennender Sorge* (*With Consuming Concern*). In this document, he spoke of the Nazis' utter rejection of peace and their distortion of the treaty with the Vatican. He alluded to the paganism inherent in arrogantly elevating a person (i.e., Hitler) or a people to the level of heaven. He further emphasized the universality of humanity as created by God and the Church's ultimate rejection of racism. Much of the document was an exhortation to the faithful of the Church to cling heroically to Christian teaching despite the trials they might face in the current and coming circumstances. In a number of public statements, he made clear his opposition to Nazism. Pope Pius proceeded to break with the Italian fascists in 1938, and he is said to have been working on a statement against anti-Semitism at the time of his death, but because of his death, it was never published.

With the outbreak of war, Archbishop Roncalli had the opportunity to undertake far more significant work in Turkey than would otherwise have been the case. Neutral Istanbul, like Bogart's Casablanca, was a hotbed of intrigue during WWII. In such a setting, Archbishop Roncalli found ways to do his part and more. He was extremely active in saving Jews from the Nazi onslaught, which will be discussed further below. In addition, he established an office for locating prisoners of war, certainly a torment he understood personally because of his family's experience during WWI. He was further able to achieve a humanitarian lifting of the Allied blockade of Greece so that food shipments could get through during the winter famine of 1941. The latter effort won a tremendous amount of goodwill towards the Catholic nuncio from an Orthodox country that was normally quite chary of the Catholic Church.

Given his prior minor postings, Archbishop Roncalli was extremely surprised when at the end of 1944 he was appointed to a vital position: papal nuncio to France, which had just been liberated from Nazi Germany. The previous nuncio was viewed as a collaborator, having been close to the Vichy head of state, General Philippe Pétain. Consequently, Archbishop Roncalli was entering an extremely sensitive situation in a critical venue. The good-natured Roncalli was deemed the right sort of person to defuse the hostile mood, reestablish the Church's independence, and negotiate the release of German seminarians being held as prisoners of war. Subsequently, he was named the first permanent Vatican observer to UNESCO, addressing its sixth and seventh general assemblies in 1951 and 1952. In that position, he enthusiastically encouraged cross-cultural dialogue and assistance.

His success with these difficult tasks was rewarded; he was elevated to a cardinal and appointed Patriarch of Venice by Pius XII in January 1953. Cardinal Roncalli was now 71 and settling into a happy old age. He probably expected Venice to be his last post. Instead, he became pope.

Electing a New Pope

The nineteen-year reign of Pius XII was at an end, and Pope John XXIII was elected to his position on October 20, 1958. With WWII barely in the past, Europe was now overshadowed and divided by the Iron Curtain. When Cardinal Roncalli was elected by a conclave of fifty-one cardinals on the twelfth ballot, it was clear to all knowledgeable observers that he was a compromise candidate. What no one expected was that his election would be a watershed moment in the long history of the Church.

The New Pope

Certainly no person knows whether their time ahead will be long or short, but at age 77, the new pope had every reason to wonder if there would be time for him to do more than merely set the course that he desired for the Church. He surprised everyone by taking the name John, the first pope with that name in more than 500 years. The last had been the antipope, John XXIII. This led to some initial confusion about what number would follow his name until he settled the matter. Angelo Roncalli took the name of John in honor of his father Giovanni and in honor of the many churches and cathedrals named after John the Baptist and John the Evangelist, including the small one in which he had been baptized—but he also pointed out that it was a name belonging to many popes with short reigns.

Pope John made it clear in his first public address as pope that he intended to be a pastoral pope. He then lost no time in working to establish an agenda. It came as a shock to those around him that his goal was nothing less than renewal of the Church. Within his first three months as pope, he announced that he would hold a diocesan synod for Rome (the first in the history of Rome was held in 1960), convene an ecumenical council (a general meeting of bishops), and revise the Code of Canon Law. The heart of his plan was a more accessible Church, one in which laypeople would not hold a second-class place.

While his horrified assistants tried to bury the plan for a new ecumenical council in a decade of preparations, the new pope made it happen within months.

The Second Vatican Council

And so, on October 11, 1962, more than 2,500 bishops from all over the world met at St. Peter's, and the Second Vatican Council began. The bishops would meet for the next four years (1962–1965), approximately four months each year, and they would change forever the way the Church operated. Pope John was able to preside over the first session.

Church Councils—and there have been very few in the course of Church history—were usually convened to correct false doctrines that were becoming popular. Pope John made it clear that his was to be a positive Church Council rather than a negative one. He was not interested in merely creating a new statement about Orthodoxy. Instead, his goal was to "open the windows" to the Church to let in fresh air and to allow a "new Pentecost." He sought, with the guidance of the Holy Spirit, to create an *aggiornamento*, an updating.

For many years predating the reign of Pope John, the Church had been fighting a losing battle against the modern world. Several popes had forcefully positioned themselves as conservative bulwarks against modern thinking. In addition, in his elder years, Pope Pius XII had increasingly isolated himself from the rest of the Curia, issuing orders by telephone but seldom listening to responses from those charged with administering the Church. As a result, there were many leaders within the

Church who were more than ready for reform and quite responsive to Pope John's call for *aggiornamento*.

In seeking Christian unity, he was prepared to acknowledge the Catholic Church's part in the Christian schism. Accordingly, he invited Eastern Orthodox, Anglican, and Protestant observers to the council.

As part of this process, in 1963 Pope John established the Pontifical Commission for the Revision of the Code of Canon Law.

The outcome, which occurred after John's death, was sixteen documents: three declarations, four constitutions, and nine decrees. In the end, traditionalists were able to modify many of the progressive changes Pope John had desired. Nevertheless, the liturgy was thoroughly revised, there was a new emphasis on ecumenism, and the Church was now fully engaged with the modern world.

Other Bold Steps

Ever since the final seizure of the Papal States and the capture of Rome by the newly unified Kingdom of Italy in 1870, the movement of popes had been severely circumscribed. Popes from Pius IX (known as Pio Nino) onward were known as prisoners in the Vatican because they refused to leave the premises, intending to make clear to all that they rejected the Italian government's authority. The Italian government, for its part, asserted that authority by placing Italian troops in front of St. Peter's Basilica. Even though Pius XI finally agreed to terms with the secular Italian state in the Lateran Treaty of 1929, which created the state of Vatican City and provided a monetary settlement for the ceded papal lands, he seldom ventured out. His successor, Pius XII, was far too protective of his papal dignity ever to mingle with the general populace—even his closest associates had to approach him on their knees. Lay workers in the Vatican were advised to make themselves scarce if he appeared.

Yet on Christmas Day 1958 Pope John stepped forth from the Vatican and became the first pope since 1870 to make pastoral visits in his own diocese of Rome. He visited two hospitals followed on the next day by a visit to a prison. There, he told the hardened but now weeping inmates that he was their brother, and he embraced a murderer. In addition, he gave the first papal press conference. Unused to such access, the public was both greatly surprised and greatly pleased. With such high visibility, the new pope very quickly began to endear himself to both Catholics and non-Catholics. Through making regular forays into poverty-stricken neighborhoods to speak with the people, he came to be popularly known as "the good pope."

Early in 1959 he ordered the words "unbelieving" and "perfidious," which were used with reference to Jews and Muslims, to be deleted from the Good Friday liturgy. Additional outreach followed. A pope had not met with the Archbishop of Canterbury for 400 years, ever since Elizabeth I had been excommunicated. Pope John met in the Vatican with the current Archbishop of Canterbury, the Most Rev. Geoffrey Francis Fisher, for approximately an hour on December 2, 1960. Then, for the first time in history, a Shinto high priest was received by a pope.

Cardinal Augustin Bea became the pope's point man for building bridges with non-Catholic communities. In January 1962 Augustin Cardinal Bea met with representatives of sixteen different religions in an unprecedented effort to overcome past hostilities. This was just one portent of the coming statement on ecumenical relations that would later emerge from Vatican II, *Nostra Aetate, Declaration on the Relation of the Church to Non-Christian Religions*, which was proclaimed by Pope Paul VI on October 28, 1965.

Although it reached its final form after the death of Pope John, *Nostra Aetate* largely accorded with the tone and process John had begun. When John died so soon into the Vatican II process, the world waited and wondered whether Vatican II would continue. His successor, Pope Paul VI, quickly reconvened the assembly and made it clear that the work was to proceed in its previously established spirit.

Nostra Aetate inaugurated a sea change in the Vatican's approach to the world because it acknowledged the sincerity and validity of other religions' quests for the divine. In keeping with Pope John's own approach, it sought commonality among the peoples of the world rather than emphasizing their differences and disputes. As Christianity's closest sibling and rival, Judaism received the most attention (more below), but Hinduism, Buddhism, and Islam also received special mention. Instead of simplistically condemning Hinduism as paganism or polytheism, *Nostra Aetate* took the more sophisticated step of recognizing Hinduism's "spiritual effort [to] contemplate the divine mystery and express it through an inexhaustible abundance of myths and through searching philosophical inquiry." Buddhism received appreciation for realizing the "radical insufficiency of this changeable world" and for its devout desire for illumination. Muslims were addressed "with esteem." Their devotion to God was applauded, along with the points of contact or proximity they held with Catholicism. Rather than apologizing for past Church behavior or seeking such an apology from Muslims, *Nostra Aetate* suggested that it would be more profitable if both parties were to forget past battles and move forward in a better spirit.

With the promulgation of *Nostra Aetate*, the Church embarked upon the path of "dialogue and collaboration." It forcefully rejected all forms of bigotry when it stated:

"'He who does not love does not know God' (1 John 4:8). No foundation therefore remains for any theory or practice that leads to discrimination between man and man or people and people, so far as their human dignity and the rights flowing from it are concerned. The Church reproves, as foreign to the mind of Christ, any discrimination against men or harassment of them because of their race, color, condition of life, or religion."

Despite the tenacity of Cardinal Bea and the support of Pope Paul VI, the document underwent considerable change before it reached its final formulation. Neither Pope John nor Pope Paul, nor even Cardinal Bea, imposed his will upon a reluctant council. Instead, it must be recalled that more than 2,000 prelates participated, and there was strong desire among a great many of them for reform. Ultimately, however, the wording of *Nostra Aetate* was produced by committee and modified under strenuous conservative pressure. As powerful a statement as it is, one can only wonder whether it might have had a different form had John lived.

Nostra Aetate began a process that continues today. Many believe that when the Church engages in triumphalism, it diminishes its core message of Christ's love and concern for all humanity. According to this view, only by recognizing our common humanity and the full breadth of humanity's striving after God—even when that striving runs counter to Church doctrine—does the Church remain faithful to the Gospels. Any teachings that run counter to this view are misrepresentations or distortions of the Gospel.

Still, not all parts of the Church have accepted the ecumenical process, the authority of the popes since Vatican II, or the authority of the Ecumenical Council known as Vatican II. Even so, many who have rejected Vatican II are still viewed as Catholics in good standing.

Another key area of John's endeavors was his activism on the world stage. Whereas Pope John held a private audience with the son-in-law of Nikita Khrushchev, he excommunicated Fidel

Castro on January 3, 1962, in accordance with a 1949 decree by Pius XII forbidding Catholics from supporting Communist governments. Although Pius made that pronouncement, he himself has been criticized for never having taken the stand of excommunicating the head of the Third Reich. Pope John, on the other hand, boldly asserted his moral authority.

Additional Measures

With his forays into prisons and hospitals and late night walks about Rome, Pope John immediately introduced a more open papal style. He took his mission as head of the Diocese of Rome very seriously and was more active and accessible within the diocese than past popes had been. This was in keeping with his affable personality and focus on pastoral responsibilities.

Setting the tone for the popes who would follow him, he ignored many of the monarchic trappings of the papacy. He rarely wore the tiara and preferred practical shoes to the more usual silk slippers. Vatican officials were no longer required to approach the pope by bowing three times and addressing him on their knees. Nor did they need to leave the room backwards. Pope John roamed the Vatican exploring and making friends with everyone from gardeners to bureaucrats. He used mealtimes as social opportunities to meet with people he needed or wanted to see.

Under Pope Pius, the number of cardinals had severely dwindled. One of Pope John's first acts was to annul a regulation dating to Sixtus IV limiting the number of members of the College of Cardinals to seventy. He enlarged it to eighty-seven, which created the largest international representation in history, including the first ever black cardinal, who was named to Dar-es-Salaam, Tanzania. For the first time, cardinals were also appointed in Mexico, Japan, and the Philippines. He consecrated fourteen indigenous bishops for Africa, Asia, and Oceania, affirming his position that colonialism needed to be dismantled and its aftermath addressed and rectified.

Among his other measures, Pope John elevated the Pontifical Commission for Cinema, Radio, and Television to curial status, approved a new code of rubrics for the Breviary and Missal, created a new Secretariat for Promoting Christian Unity (this was the group headed by Cardinal Bea, which actually had more to do with non-Christian groups than the title would indicate), and appointed the first Vatican representative to the Assembly of the World Council of Churches held in New Delhi in 1961. This new association with the World Council of Churches constituted the Vatican's first positive recognition of Protestant Christianity and the need to work together cooperatively with non-Catholic Christians.

Pope John's Message

Pope John wrote eight encyclicals, two of which are considered to have been particularly groundbreaking: *Mater et Magistra* (*Mother and Teacher*) in 1961 and *Pacem en Terris* (*Peace on Earth*), which was promulgated only two months before his death in 1963.

Mater et Magistra was issued in 1961 to commemorate the anniversary of Pope Leo XIII's *Rerum Novarum* (*On Capital and Labor*), which upheld the dignity and rights of workers. The young Angelo had first arrived at the seminary in Bergamo in the year following the 1891 issuance of Leo's encyclical, and in that city he had witnessed firsthand the progressive Catholic social action that ensued: soup kitchens, demonstrations, and the organization of Catholic unions and credit associations. Now Pope John built upon Leo's support of workers by declaring the Catholic Church's interest in the earthly existence of humanity as a whole, the "exigencies of man's daily life, with his livelihood and education, and his general, temporal welfare and prosperity."

Pacem in Terris advocated human freedom and dignity as the basis for world order and peace.

Pope John might have been less optimistic had he known how intransigent so many social and global problems would prove to be. Today we also know that the earth's capacity for self-renewal is far from infinite. It is important to recognize that at the time John was writing, there was not yet an organized environmental movement; Rachel Carson's seminal work, *Silent Spring*, was first published in 1962. The crisis of global overpopulation by humans was not yet fully appreciated. Moreover, the experiment known as the welfare state was only beginning to be launched. Pope John believed in addressing practical situations in realistic terms. Had he lived for another few decades, his views might have been different.

Pope John and the Liturgy

Although he supported the use of vernacular in some circumstances, Pope John ardently defended the virtues of Latin as a native treasure of the Latin Church. He extolled its linguistic precision as the perfect vehicle for logical thought, and he somewhat naively wanted it preserved as the means of communication between the international components of the Church. He insisted that it be the language of Vatican II, but the reality was that many of the prelates present simply could not communicate effectively in Latin.

Pope John and Women

At the time he was secretary to Bishop Radini-Tadeschi, Father Angelo was afforded the opportunity to work with several women's groups. Monsignor Radini created three organizations to aid women: the League of Women Workers, the Association for the Protection of Young Women, and the Casa di Maternità. Father Angelo was made an advisor to these women's groups. He also became president of the women's section of Catholic Action in the diocese.

It is probably not fair to expect from a man of Pope John's vintage too much more than was typical of his contemporaries. Having said that, his kindness and good sense led him to sometimes surprising remarks.

In an important letter directed to women religious, he reinforced their roles as either contemplative or active Sisters ("Letter of Pope John XXIII 'Il Tempe Massimo' to Women Religious," July 2, 1962). He was quite emphatic about maintaining the traditional values of poverty, chastity, and obedience and the redemptive function of prayer for the Church as a whole. Still, he opened for them the door to the life of the mind. He warned them not to close themselves to modern scientific discoveries, social and political movements, or cultural conventions, because these matters were important even to cloistered religious.

He further encouraged active religious women to obtain the education and degrees necessary to aid them in their work. It must be remembered that higher education for women at the beginning of the 1960s was by no means a given. Nevertheless, he viewed their work as being within the traditional confines of "education, charity, and social service."

Pope John and the Jews

One of Pope John's most honorable achievements is his undoing of nearly 2,000 years of what French-Jewish historian Jules Isaac (who had lost his own wife and daughter in Auschwitz) called "the teaching of contempt" by the Church.

It is not known why Angelo Roncalli felt such a kinship with the Jewish people and was so willing to act on their behalf, but it was a measure of the greatness of his heart that he did. In his youth at the seminary in Rome, he won an award for excellence in Hebrew language studies. Later, at his various professional posts, he made many Jewish friends. During his brief time as pope, he granted approximately 120 private audiences to Jewish persons and groups. Both before and after becoming pope, he arguably did more to save Jewish lives and improve relations with the Jewish people than any Catholic in history.

The full extent of his life-saving activity during the Holocaust may never be known. While his appointment to Turkey and Greece was frustrating in many ways, it positioned him to become an activist in rescue efforts during WWII. Using his many contacts, there is no question that he saved the lives of many tens of thousands of Jews. Certainly, he was entirely forthright in stating his views at the time.

When the devoutly Catholic German ambassador, Franz von Papen, suggested to him that the anti-Communist Pope Pius XII should publicly support Germany's invasion of the Soviet Union, the archbishop bluntly responded, "And what shall I tell the Holy Father about the thousands of Jews who have died in Germany and Poland at the hands of your countrymen?" Later, when von Papen stood trial at Nuremburg, the archbishop communicated to the tribunal that von Papen had helped him save 24,000 Jews, presumably by looking the other way.

Sadly, Archbishop Roncalli's repeated requests for Vatican intercession and his recommendations for Vatican action in very specific, concrete situations when action might have made a world of difference usually fell on deaf ears. On one occasion, however, he seems to have been successful in prompting the Vatican to action. Having met with the Chief Rabbi of Jerusalem, Isaac Herzog, concerning the tens of thousands of Jews stranded in Transnistria (having been deported from other nearby regions), he was able to convince the Vatican to intercede with the fascist Romanian government, which was occupying the district, on their behalf. There is little indication that it helped; most of the Jews trapped in the region would perish.

Nonetheless, the archbishop's own personal interventions were more consistently successful. When Jewish refugees first began arriving in Istanbul, they sought an audience with the archbishop, seeking his assistance. Although he had heard reports through the clerical grapevine, it was in this way that he became directly aware of what was happening under Nazi and fascist rule. When necessary, he now provided clothing and money to refugees in transit, but he had a greater impact in a different way. Working with Chaim Birlas, head of the Palestine Jewish Agency's Rescue Committee, he sent large quantities of Vatican visas and so-called immigration certificates issued by the Jewish Agency to Romania and Hungary.

He was helped in this endeavor by the papal nuncio in Budapest, Angelo Ratti, who in turn was working with Swedish diplomat Raoul Wallenberg. The documents lacked real legal authority, but they looked official and helped many to escape to then-British Palestine. There may even have been false baptismal certificates issued; at least, a legend has grown up to that effect. The documents were transported using diplomatic couriers, Vatican representatives, and the Sisters of Our Lady of Zion. It is believed that the number of adults and children saved in this way may have amounted to tens of thousands.

The archbishop's prior contacts in Bulgaria also came into play when he made a request to King Boris of Bulgaria, who was allied with the Axis powers, to allow the Red Cross to save thousands of Slovakian Jews in Bulgarian-occupied lands. Boris supported the deportation of Jews from Bulgarian-occupied lands in Greek and Yugoslav territories and from Bulgaria itself, but a rising tide of protests in Bulgaria, including from the Metropolitan of the Bulgarian Orthodox Church, caused some delays and a change in tactics.

Few people in that terrible time did as much to save Jewish lives as the gentle, affable, and largely ignored Archbishop Roncalli. He called the murder of Jews during the war "six million crucifixions." Still, he did not seek public commendation for his efforts and is thus best known for what followed.

For two millennia the Church had done much to ensure that Jews suffered and then attributed this suffering to God's just retribution. The imagery of "abject Judea" was rife within pre-modern Europe. For a Church steeped in triumphalism, the reemergence of Israel as a political entity was an awkward fact that was best ignored.

Now, however, Pope John signaled a thawing of relations between the Vatican and the Jewish people, and he did so very early in his tenure. Israeli President Yitzchak Ben Zvi was included among the heads of state to whom papal letters of accession were sent by this newly elected pope. This is in marked contrast to John's friend and successor, Paul VI, who, when making a pilgrimage to the Holy Land in 1964, would refuse to address the Israeli president (Zalman Shazar) by his title.

With the revelations about the fate of Europe's Jews that came in the wake of WWII, there were sporadic, localized attempts by Church figures to address the Church's role through its teaching of contempt. In 1949 Pius XII had in a limited way addressed the use of *pro perfidis Judaeis* in the Good Friday prayer for the Jews by allowing the phrase to be translated in its actual meaning of "unfaithful" or "unbelieving" instead of the even more insidious translation of "perfidious," which was how it had usually been translated. John XXIII very quickly, in 1959, eliminated the word altogether along with harsh statements in two other prayers: the Act of Consecration to the Sacred Heart and the baptism of converts ritual. In place of the long-standing but dubious invocation to pray for the *perfidis Judaeis*, he instituted a genuinely benevolent petition asking that Jews remain faithful to their covenant and continue to love God's name. He further ordered an end to pilgrimage to a shrine in Daggendorf, Bavaria, where thousands converged annually to celebrate the 1338 massacre of the town's Jewish community.

It was Vatican II, however, that provided an organized forum for working out policy towards Jews and other non-Catholics, including Hindus, Buddhists, Muslims, and non-Catholic Christians. Historically, preparations for the council occurred concurrently with the Eichmann trial in Jerusalem (1961). Adolph Eichmann was considered to be the architect of Hitler's "Final Solution," and media coverage of his 14-week trial brought to the public ongoing, horrific, and vivid testimony about the inhumanity that had occurred only a few years earlier. While some Catholics preferred to focus on the extent to which Catholics had rendered aid to Jews, others were engaged in intense soul-searching about the history of Catholic animosity (and Christian animosity in general) toward Jews that had helped give rise to modern anti-Semitism.

Accordingly, *Nostra Aetate* may be the most notable document to emerge from Vatican II, albeit after John's death, because it altered Catholic perceptions of the Jewish people forever. Mindful of the "spiritual patrimony" shared by Christians and Jews, it overturned 2,000 years of Church history by stating:

"The Jews should not be presented as rejected or accursed by God, as if this followed from the Holy Scriptures…Furthermore, in her rejection of every persecution against any man, the Church, mindful of the patrimony she shares with the Jews and moved not by political reasons but by the Gospel's spiritual love, decries hatred, persecutions, displays of anti-Semitism, directed against Jews at any time and by anyone."

These and other such statements resulted in a complete, systematic overhaul of Catholic textbooks and approaches to teaching about non-Catholics. Most importantly, *Nostra Aetate* removed the charge of deicide and caused this and other such historical distortions to be removed from Catholic liturgy and teachings. Under Pope Paul VI, *Nostra Aetate* was followed in January 1975 by *Guidelines for the Implementation of Nostra Aetate No. 4*. These guidelines were a further advance over *Nostra Aetate* because they referenced the Holocaust and also Judaism's ongoing religious tradition beyond the destruction of Jerusalem. (Christianity has often treated Judaism as though its viability ended at that point.) The guidelines included other important points as well. What they still failed to acknowledge was the centrality of the land of Israel within Jewish belief.

Pope John had paved the way for *Nostra Aetate* by charging Cardinal Bea with the task of crafting a statement on Catholic–Jewish relations and seeking Jewish viewpoints about the subject. The door was thus opened for Catholic–Jewish engagement. Pope John fully supported Cardinal Bea's activities in the face of intense religious opposition from conservative elements within the Church and politically motivated opposition from Arab governments outside it. Nevertheless, the "Declaration on the Jews" drafted by Cardinal Bea was shelved for the duration of Pope John's lifetime. Pope John died only two months after the first session of Vatican II. The subject would be taken up again only thereafter.

Death

In his will dated September 12, 1961, Pope John spoke confidently of "Sister Death." Sadly, this sweet, loving man would not know an easy death, but there is no question that he would have dedicated his suffering to heaven and made it an atonement for his flock. In September 1962 Pope John was diagnosed with stomach cancer. There had been intermittent signs of illness during the preceding eight months. Now the diagnosis was kept from the public, but the pope grew increasingly wan while his public appearances diminished. His pain at times was excruciating.

Even while undergoing his final trial, Pope John helped eased the tensions of the Cuban Missile Crisis when he offered to mediate between President Kennedy and Premier Nikita Khrushchev at the end of 1962. Both parties appreciated the gesture.

In January 1963, Pope John was *Time's* Man of the Year because of his "New Pentecost" that was reorienting the Church towards the modern world.

Pope John made what would be his last public appearance on May 11, 1963, when Italian president Antonio Segni awarded him with the Balzan Prize for his work on behalf of peace. He attended despite being in tremendous pain. On May 25, he experienced hemorrhaging and received blood transfusions. The cancer, however, had perforated the stomach wall, causing peritonitis. The pope's assistant, Loris Capovilla, told him that the cancer "had done its work," and nothing could be done. The pope's remaining siblings rallied around him.

On May 31, Pope John spoke what are considered his final words: "I had the great grace to be born into a Christian family, modest and poor, but with the fear of the Lord. My time on earth is drawing to a close. But Christ lives on and continues his work in the Church. Souls, souls, That they might all be one [*Ut omnes unum sint*]." The Papal Sacristan then performed the final unction but became so emotional that he forgot the correct order for anointing. The pope gently guided him. Pope John XXIII died at 7:49 p.m. Roman time on June 3, 1963, just as a mass for him was finishing below in Saint Peter's Square below. He was 81 years old.

Pope John was proud of his peasant origins. At his death, he wanted the same honor as that which was bestowed on Pius X: that people could say of him he was born poor and died poor. He believed poverty to be the first duty of anyone following Jesus ("Letter of Pope John XXIII 'Il Tempio Massimo' to Women Religious," July 2, 1962). Accordingly, when he bequeathed to his surviving family members the whole of his worldly wealth, it amounted to less than $20 apiece. He was buried beneath St.

Peter's Basilica. Two wreaths were lovingly donated by prisoners in Italian jails.

At the time Pope John was elected, another candidate had been the Archbishop of Milan, Giovanni Battista Montini. Archbishop Montini, however, had not yet been named a cardinal, and the College of Cardinals usually chose someone from among their own number. Upon his election, Pope John quickly rectified the situation; he elevated Montini to a cardinal only one month after he became pope. With the death of Pope John, Cardinal Montini became his successor, Pope Paul VI. He quickly affirmed that he would continue the process begun by Pope John.

Legacy

John XXIII was nicknamed "The Good Pope" because of his humble, loving, and open character and his gracious sense of humor. In possessing those attributes, he is viewed by many to be similar to Pope Francis today. Like Pope Francis, Pope John was wont to stroll about Rome by night and make pastoral visits to sick children and prison inmates. John's secretary, the Italian prelate Loris Capovilla, heard the news from Pope Francis himself and remarked how appropriate it was for the step to be taken by "the successor most similar" to John. "He reminds me in every way of John XXIII: in his gestures, in his attention to the poor...He has the same humility and mildness of heart as John XXIII, who was a wise and enlightened father who spoke to the human family that is torn apart by opposing interests and by senseless and sometimes implacable dislikes."

The crowning feature of John's papacy was his calling the Second Vatican Council (1962–1965) into existence. The Council would revise the Church's rituals and doctrines, reach out to other faiths in dialogue and good will, and raise the status of lay people. Pope Francis has explained the significance of Vatican II in this way: "Vatican II was a re-reading of the gospel in light of contemporary culture...[It] produced a renewal movement that simply comes from the same gospel. Its fruits are enormous. Just recall the liturgy. The work of liturgical reform has been a service to the people as a re-reading of the gospel from a concrete historical situation."

Shortly before Pope John's death, the International Balzan Foundation, which is headquartered in Milan and Zurich, awarded Pope John its Peace Prize. Then, in December 1963, President Lyndon Johnson posthumously awarded him the United States' Presidential Medal of Freedom, the nation's highest civilian award.

Pope John XXIII was beatified by Pope John Paul II in 2000 with one miracle to his credit, the case of an Italian nun with hemorrhaging. His body was then moved from its original burial place in the grottoes beneath St. Peter's Basilica to near the main altar. His feast date is October 11 to commemorate the opening of Vatican II.

The canonization of Pope John XXIII was announced by Pope Francis shortly after the fiftieth anniversary of John's death. The date for canonization has been set for April 27, 2014, Divine Mercy Sunday, the first Sunday after Easter. It will occur together with that of Pope John Paul II, the first time that two people have been canonized together. This is fitting because of the way the two figures bracket the process of Vatican II; if John inaugurated Vatican II, John Paul was both a product and a proponent of that process. By canonizing both simultaneously, it is believed the Vatican wants to highlight the unity of the process despite any perceived differences between John's supposed liberalism and John Paul's conservatism. The date for the occasion was originally scheduled for December 8; however, the Polish bishops complained that it would be difficult for many Poles to attend at the time because of inclement winter conditions.

It is unusual for canonization to occur with only one miracle in place; however, Pope Francis has called witness to John's "heroic virtue" as the basis for moving forward with canonization. There may also have been a popular clamor among the participants in Vatican II for the canonization to occur.

And, after all, the canonization ceremony is only a recognition and confirmation of what has already been decided at the divine level.

The Rosary

Pope John XXIII said, "The Rosary is a magnificent and universal prayer for the needs of the Church, the nations and the entire world." In fact, Pope John XXIII spoke 38 times about our Lady and the Rosary. He prayed 15 decades daily.

Like Pope John XXIII, and Pope John Paul II, Pope Francis has stressed the importance of the rosary.

In a September 2013 interview, Pope Francis discussed his daily prayers, stating, "I pray the breviary every morning. I like to pray with the psalms. Then, later, I celebrate Mass. I pray the Rosary. What I really prefer is adoration in the evening, even when I get distracted and think of other things, or even fall asleep praying. In the evening then, between seven and eight o'clock, I stay in front of the Blessed Sacrament for an hour in adoration. But I pray mentally even when I am waiting at the dentist or at other times of the day."

A month earlier, at the Mass for the Assumption of the Blessed Virgin Mary, Pope Francis urged Catholics to pray the rosary, "Mary joins us, she fights at our side. She supports Christians in the fight against the forces of evil. Especially through prayer, through the rosary. Hear me out, the rosary... Do you pray the Rosary each day? I don't know, are you sure? There we go!"

As a child, I remember seeing my grandmother pray the rosary. I remember thinking that the practice was odd, even frightening to watch. Often we are afraid of things that we do not understand, and I have since learned that the tradition of praying the rosary is quite beautiful. I hope the following chapter provides both instruction and reference for practicing Catholics, and a deeper understanding for those of different religions. The following chapter explains in detail the traditions of praying the rosary, a tradition that Pope Francis holds dear.

The following sections provide a brief overview of how to pray the rosary. This section also appears in The Life and Legacy of Pope John Paul II & Pope Francis, by Wyatt North and Michael Ruszala respectively.

First, begin by holding the cross and repeating the "Sign of the Cross."

Sign of the Cross

In The Name of the Father and of the Son and of the Holy Spirit.

Then, "The Apostle's Creed" is said on the Cross.

The Apostle's Creed

I believe in God, the Father Almighty, Creator of heaven and earth and in Jesus Christ, His only Son, our Lord; Who was conceived by the Holy Spirit, born of the Virgin Mary, suffered under Pontius Pilate, was crucified, died, and was buried, He descended into hell; the third day He arose again from the dead; He ascended into Heaven, sitteth at the right hand of God, the Father Almighty, from thence He shall come to judge the living and the dead. I believe in the Holy Spirit, the Holy Catholic Church, the communion of saints, the forgiveness of sins, the resurrection of the body, and life everlasting. Amen.

Next, on the single bead just above the cross, pray the "Our Father." Remember, Rosary prayers are considered Meditative prayers as opposed to personal prayers. In personal prayer the prayer speaks to God. In meditative prayer we allow God to speak to us through his word and his Spirit.

Our Father

Our Father, Who art in Heaven, hallowed be Thy name; Thy Kingdom come, Thy will be done on earth as it is in Heaven. Give us this day our daily bread; and forgive us our trespasses as we forgive those who trespass against us; and lead us not into temptation, but deliver us from evil. Amen.

The next cluster on the rosary has 3 beads. With this group of beads, the prayer should recite the "Hail Mary." The prayer should recite 3 Hail Marys while allowing God to speak through his words on the three divine virtues of faith, hope, and love.

Hail Mary

Hail Mary, full of grace, the Lord is with thee, blessed art thou amongst women and blessed is the fruit of thy womb, Jesus. Holy Mary Mother of God, pray for us sinners now and at the hour of our death. Amen.

Repeat this three times.

After the three beads, there is a chain. Hold the bare chain and recite the "Glory be to the Father" prayer.

Glory be to the Father

Glory be to the Father, the Son, and the Holy Spirit.

The next bead is a single bead. Hold this bead in your hand and say the divine mystery of contemplation. For example, if it were a Monday or a Saturday, you would say the first Joyful Mystery, "The Annunciation."

The First Joyful Mystery: The Annunciation of the Angel Gabriel to Mary (Lk 1:26-38)

In the sixth month, the angel Gabriel was sent from God to a town of Galilee called Nazareth, to a virgin betrothed to a man named Joseph, of the house of David, and the virgin's name was Mary. And coming to her, he said, "Hail, favored one! The Lord is with you." But she was greatly troubled at what was said and pondered what sort of greeting this might be. Then the angel said to her, "Do not be afraid, Mary, for you have found favor with God. Behold, you will conceive in your womb and bear a son, and you shall name him Jesus. He will be great and will be called Son of the Most High, and the Lord God will give him the throne of David his father, and he will rule over the house of Jacob forever, and of his kingdom there will be no end." But Mary said to the angel, "How can this be, since I have no relations with a man?" And the angel said to her in reply, "The Holy Spirit will come upon you, and the power of the Most High will overshadow you. Therefore the child to be born will be called holy, the Son of God. And behold, Elizabeth, your relative, has also conceived a son in her old age, and this is the sixth month for her who was called barren; for nothing will be impossible for God." Mary said, "Behold, I am the handmaid of the Lord. May it be done to me according to your word." Then the angel departed from her.

Then you may prayer the "Our Father" prayer for the second time.

Our Father

Our Father, Who art in Heaven, hallowed be Thy name; Thy Kingdom come, Thy will be done on earth as it is in Heaven. Give us this day our daily bread; and forgive us our trespasses as we forgive those who trespass against us; and lead us not into temptation, but deliver us from evil. Amen.

This brings you to a set of ten beads on the rosary. You should then pray 10 Hail Marys while contemplating the first mystery. The example of The Annunciation is provided above.

Hail Mary

Hail Mary, full of grace, the Lord is with thee, blessed art thou amongst women and blessed is the fruit of thy womb, Jesus. Holy Mary Mother of God, pray for us sinners now and at the hour of our death. Amen.

Repeat this ten times.

After the 10th Hail Mary you will have completed the first of 5 decades. The next section of the rosary, is a single bead. Repeat the "Glory be to the Father."

Glory be to the Father

Glory Be to the Father, the Son, and the Holy Spirit.

Next, on the same bead, pray the "O My Jesus."

O My Jesus

O My Jesus, have mercy on us. Forgive us our sins. Save us from the fires of hell. Take all souls into heaven, especially, those most in need of thy mercy. Amen.

Then, on the same bead, announce the next or second mystery. For example: if it is Monday and your praying the Joyful Mysteries, the second Joyful Mystery is The Visitation.

The Second Joyful Mystery: The Visitation of Mary to Elizabeth (Lk 1:39-50)

During those days Mary set out and traveled to the hill country in haste to a town of Judah, where she entered the house of Zechariah and greeted Elizabeth. When Elizabeth heard Mary's greeting, the infant leaped in her womb, and Elizabeth, filled with the Holy Spirit, cried out in a loud voice and said, "Most blessed are you among women, and blessed is the fruit of your womb. And how does this happen to me, that the mother of my Lord should come to me? For at the moment the sound of your greeting reached my ears, the infant in my womb leaped for joy. Blessed are you who believed that what was spoken to you by the Lord would be fulfilled." And Mary said: "My soul proclaims the greatness of the Lord; my spirit rejoices in God my savior. For he has looked upon his handmaid's lowliness; behold, from now on will all ages call me blessed. The Mighty One has done great things for me, and holy is his name. His mercy is from age to age to those who fear him...."

Next, repeat the "Our Father."

Our Father

Our Father, Who art in Heaven, hallowed be Thy name; Thy
Kingdom come, Thy will be done on earth as it is in Heaven. Give
us this day our daily bread; and forgive us our trespasses as we
forgive those who trespass against us; and lead us not into
temptation, but deliver us from evil.   Amen.

If you enjoyed Pope Francis: The Good Pope, you might also enjoy our original biography of Pope Francis, entitled Pope Francis: Pastor of Mercy. Please enjoy the first two chapters on the following pages.

Introduction

There is something about Pope Francis that captivates and delights people, even people who hardly know anything about him. He was elected in only two days of the conclave, yet many who tried their hand at speculating on who the next pope may be barely included him on their lists. The evening of Wednesday, March 13, 2013, the traditional white smoke poured out from the chimney of the Sistine Chapel and spread throughout the world by way of television, Internet, radio, and social media, signaling the beginning of a new papacy. As the light of day waned from the Eternal City, some 150,000 people gathered watching intently for any movement behind the curtained door to the loggia of St. Peter's. A little after 8:00 p.m., the doors swung open and Cardinal Tauran emerged to pronounce the traditional and joyous Latin formula to introduce the new Bishop of Rome: "Annuncio vobis gaudium magnum; habemus papam!" ("I announce to you a great joy: we have a pope!") He then announced the new Holy Father's identity: "Cardinalem Bergoglio..."

The name Bergoglio, stirred up confusion among most of the faithful who flooded the square that were even more clueless than the television announcers were, who scrambled to figure out who exactly the new pope was. Pausing briefly, Cardinal Tauran continued by announcing the name of the new pope, he said "...qui sibi nomen imposuit Franciscum" ("who takes for himself the name Francis"). Whoever this man may be, his name choice resonated with all, and the crowd erupted with jubilant cheers. A few moments passed before the television announcers and their support teams informed their global audiences that the man who was about to walk onto the loggia dressed in white was Cardinal Jorge Mario Bergoglio, age 76, of Buenos Aires, Argentina.

To add to the bewilderment and kindling curiosity, when the new pope stepped out to the thunderous applause of the crowd in St. Peter's Square, he did not give the expected papal gesture of outstretched arms. Instead, he gave only a simple and modest wave. Also, before giving his first apostolic blessing, he bowed asking the faithful, from the least to the greatest, to silently pray for him. These acts were only the beginning of many more words and gestures, such as taking a seat on the bus with the cardinals, refusing a pope mobile with bulletproof glass, and paying his own hotel bill after his election, that would raise eyebrows among some familiar with papal customs and delight the masses.

Is he making a pointed critique of previous pontificates? Is he simply posturing a persona to the world at large to make a point? The study of the life of Jorge Mario Bergoglio gives a clear answer, and the answer is no. This is simply who he is as a man and as a priest. The example of his thought provoking gestures flows from his character, his life experiences, his religious vocation, and his spirituality. This book uncovers the life of the

266th Bishop of Rome, Jorge Mario Bergoglio, also known as Father Jorge; a name he preferred even while he was an archbishop and cardinal.

What exactly do people find so attractive about Pope Francis? Aldo Cagnoli, a layman that developed a friendship with the Pope when he was serving as a cardinal, shares the following: "The greatness of the man, in my humble opinion lies not in building walls or seeking refuge behind his wisdom and office, but rather in dealing with everyone judiciously, respectfully, and with humility, being willing to learn at any moment of life; that is what Father Bergoglio means to me" (as quoted in Ch. 12 of Pope Francis: Conversations with Jorge Bergoglio, previously published as La Jesuita [The Jesuit]).

At World Youth Day 2013, in Rio de Janeiro, Brazil, three million young people came out to praise and celebrate Pope Francis. Doug Barry, from EWTN's Life on the Rock, interviewed youth at the event on what features stood out to them about Pope Francis. The young people seemed most touched by his authenticity. One young woman from St. Louis said, "He really knows his audience. He doesn't just say things to say things... And he is really sincere and genuine in all that he does." A friend agreed: "He was looking out into the crowd and it felt like he was looking at each one of us...." A young man from Canada weighed in: "You can actually relate to [him]... for example, last night he was talking about the World Cup and athletes." A young woman added, "I feel he means what he says... he practices what he preaches... he states that he's there for the poor and he actually means it."

The Holy Spirit guided the College of Cardinals in its election of Pope Francis to meet the needs of the Church following the historic resignation of Pope Benedict XVI due to old age. Representing the growth and demographic shift in the Church throughout the world and especially in the Southern Hemisphere, Pope Francis is the first non-European pope in almost 1,300 years. He is also the first Jesuit pope. Pope Francis comes with a different background and set of experiences. Both as archbishop and as pope, his flock knows him for his humility, ascetic frugality in solidarity with the poor, and closeness. He was born in Buenos Aires to a family of Italian immigrants, earned a diploma in chemistry, and followed a priestly vocation in the Jesuit order after an experience of God's mercy while receiving the sacrament of Reconciliation. Even though he is known for his smile and humor, the world also recognize Pope Francis as a stern figure that stands against the evils of the world and challenges powerful government officials, when necessary.

The Church he leads, is one that has been burdened in the West by the aftermath of sex abuse scandals and increased secularism. It is also a Church that is experiencing shifting in numbers out of the West and is being challenged with religious persecution in the Middle East, Asia, and Africa. The Vatican that Pope Francis has inherited is plagued by cronyism and scandal. This Holy Father knows, however, that his job is not merely about numbers, politics, or even success. He steers clear of pessimism knowing that he is the vicar of the Body of Christ and works with grace. This is the man God has chosen in these times to lead his flock.

Early Life in Argentina

Jorge Mario Bergoglio was born on December 17, 1936, in the Flores district of Buenos Aires. The district was a countryside locale outside the main city during the nineteenth century and many rich people in its early days called this place home. By the time Jorge was born, Flores was incorporated into the city of Buenos Aires and became a middle class neighborhood. Flores is also the home of the beautiful Romantic-styled Basilica of San José de Flores, built in 1831, with its dome over the altar, spire over the entrance, and columns at its facade. It was the Bergoglios's parish church and had much significance in Jorge's life.

Jorge's father's family had arrived in Argentina in 1929, immigrating from Piedimonte in northern Italy. They were not the only ones immigrating to the country. In the late nineteenth century, Argentina became industrialized and the government promoted immigration from Europe. During that time, the land prospered and Buenos Aires earned the moniker "Paris of the South." In the late nineteenth and early twentieth centuries waves of immigrants from Italy, Spain, and other European countries came off ships in the port of Buenos Aires. Three of Jorge's great uncles were the first in the family to immigrate to Argentina in 1922 searching for better employment opportunities after World War I. They established a paving company in Buenos Aires and built a four-story building for their company with the city's first elevator. Jorge's father and paternal grandparents followed the brothers in order to keep the family together and to escape Mussolini's fascist regime in Italy. Jorge's father and grandfather also helped with the business for a time. His father, Mario, who had been an accountant for a rail company in Italy, provided similar services for the family business (Cardinal Bergoglio recalls more on the story of his family's immigration and his early life in Ch. 1 of Conversations with Jorge Bergoglio).

Providentially, the Bergoglios were long delayed in liquidating their assets in Italy; forcing them to miss the ship they planned to sail on, the doomed Pricipessa Mafaldai, which sank off the northern coast of Brazil before reaching Buenos Aires. The family took the Giulio Cesare instead and arrived safely in Argentina with Jorge's Grandma Rosa. Grandma Rosa wore a fur coat stuffed with the money the family brought with them from Italy. Economic hard times eventually hit Argentina in 1932 and the family's paving business went under, but the Bergoglio brothers began anew.

Jorge's father, Mario, met his mother Regina at Mass in 1934. Regina was born in Argentina, but her parents were also Italian immigrants. Mario and Regina married the following year after meeting. Jorge, the eldest of their five children, was born in 1936. Jorge fondly recalls his mother gathering the children around the radio on Sunday afternoons to listen to opera and explain the story. A true porteño, as the inhabitants of the port city of Buenos Aires are called, Jorge liked to play soccer, listen to Latin music, and dance the tango. Jorge's paternal grandparents lived around the corner from his home. He greatly admired his Grandma Rosa, and keeps her written prayer for her grandchildren with him until this day. Jorge recalls that while his grandparents kept their personal conversations in Piedmontese, Mario chose mostly to speak Spanish preferring to look forward rather than back. Still, Jorge grew up speaking both Italian and Spanish.

Upon entering secondary school at the age of thirteen, his father insisted that Jorge begin work even though the family, in their modest lifestyle, was not particularly in need of extra income. Mario Bergoglio wanted to teach the boy the value of work and found several jobs for him during his adolescent years. Jorge worked in a hosiery factory for several years, as a cleaner and at a desk. When he entered technical school to study food chemistry, Jorge found a job working in a laboratory. He worked under a woman that always challenged him to do his work thoroughly. He remembers her, though, with both fondness and sorrow. Years later, she was kidnapped and murdered along with members of her family because of her political views during the Dirty War, a conflict in the 1970's and 80's between the military dictatorship and guerrilla fighters where thousands of Argentineans disappeared.

Initially unhappy with his father's decision to make him work, Jorge recalls later in his life that work was a valuable formative experience for him that taught him responsibility, realism, and how the world operated. He learned that a person's self worth often comes from their work, which led him to become committed later in life to promote a just culture of work rather than simply encouraging charity or entitlement. He believes that people need meaningful work in order to thrive. During his boyhood through his priestly ministry, he experienced the gulf in Argentina between the poor and the well off, which left the poor having few opportunities for gainful employment.

At the age of twenty-one, Jorge became dangerously ill. He was diagnosed with severe pneumonia and cysts. Part of his upper right lung was removed, and each day Jorge endured the pain and discomfort of saline fluid pumped through his chest to clear his system. Jorge remembers that the only person that was able to comfort him during this time was a religious sister who had catechized him from childhood, Sister Dolores. She exposed him to the true meaning of suffering with this simple statement: "You are imitating Christ." This stuck with him, and his sufferings during that time served as a crucible for his character, teaching him how to distinguish what is important in life from what is not. He was being prepared for what God was calling him to do in life, his vocation.

Made in the USA
Middletown, DE
08 November 2018